DARING WOMEN

~25~
WOMEN
WHO
DARED *to* COMPETE

by Rebecca Stanborough

COMPASS POINT BOOKS
a capstone imprint

Daring Women is published by Compass Point Books, an imprint of Capstone.
1710 Roe Crest Drive
North Mankato, Minnesota 56003
www.capstonepub.com

Library of Congress Cataloging-in-Publication Data is available on the Library of Congress website.
ISBN: 978-0-7565-6615-9 (hardcover)
ISBN: 978-0-7565-6659-3 (paperback)
ISBN: 978-0-7565-6623-4 (eBook PDF)

Summary: Discover 25 women who challenged the stereotypes of what it means to play like a girl. These women worked to even the playing field and stepped up to score points for women all around the world.

Image Credits
Alamy: Natural History Archive, 26; Getty Images: Barry Batchelor/PA Images, 52, Bettmann, 7, 23, 25, 31, Christian Petersen, 46, Dave Winter, 54, Jamie Squire, Cover, John Giles/PA Images, 9, Kyodo News, 15, Melissa Renwick, 27, Professional Sport, 33, RacingOne, 19, Stan Grossfeld/The Boston Globe, 51, Transcendental Graphics, 17, 49; Newscom: Darryl Dennis/Icon SMI Select, 41; Shutterstock: Debby Wong, 44, elena bee, 39, Jose Breton-Pics Action, 37, Keeton Gale, 11, KIM WONKOOK, 29, Leonard Zhukovsky, 5, 12, 35, 55, lev radin, 43, Photo Works, 20

Design Elements by Shutterstock

Editorial Credits
Editors: Peter Mavrikis and Mari Bolte ; Designer: Bobbie Nuytten;
Media Researcher: Tracy Cummins; Production Specialist: Laura Manthe

Printed in the United States of America.
PA117

TABLE OF CONTENTS

INTRODUCTION

In the era of superstars like Serena and Venus Williams, Simone Biles, and Megan Rapinoe, it's hard to imagine that our grandmothers had to fight for the right to play at all. Not long ago, in 1937, the official position of the American Physical Education Association (APEA) was that women should "play for play's sake." Competition *for girls*? Totally unnecessary.

In the 1960s, girls and women began competing against one another. Still, boys' teams were given superior facilities and equipment. And some people couldn't handle the idea of women in sports at all. In 1967, runner Kathrine Switzer was physically attacked just for trying to compete in the Boston Marathon.

Thank goodness society and progress don't stand still.

Today, the whole world has seen that women are fast, fierce, strong competitors. They can run, jump, dunk, dive, parry, and pitch. Powerful uppercuts, impossible landings, and down-to-the-buzzer goals are all part of the games women play. All across the globe, daring women sweat, break bones, tear ligaments, and keep on playing.

They have come a long way—but there are still hurdles to jump. In many sports, women are not paid the same as men. Women's games don't receive the same media coverage. And the world needs more women referees, announcers, and coaches.

But there are also many wins to celebrate. Winning championship titles and gold medals inspires us to reach further and train harder. We cheer the trailblazing women who changed their sports—and the world—forever.

“ *It's important to teach our female youth that it's OK to say, 'Yes, I am good at this,' and you don't hold back.* ”
—Simone Biles

Chapter 1

RECORD-BREAKERS: WOMEN CHAMPIONS

Competing at the highest level is hard enough. Winning—and then winning again and again—is even tougher. These women dreamed big and aimed high. Through hard work, motivation, and talent, they raced, tumbled, and hurdled their way to becoming champions.

Mildred "Babe" Didrikson Zaharias
(1911–1956)
All-Around Sports Champion

When Babe Didrikson was just a kid, she asked her neighbors to trim their hedges to the height of Olympic hurdles. Then she raced down Doucette Street, leaping over them one by one. She was dreaming of the Olympics from a very young age.

Before she reached her teens, she declared, "I am going to be the best athlete of all time." It might have seemed like empty bragging. But she tackled so many sports and won so many trophies that it seemed she was headed for that title.

In 1932, her employer sent Didrikson to compete in the U.S. women's track and field championships. Most companies sent

Babe Didrikson won three medals and set three records at the 1932 Olympic Games in Los Angeles, California. The feat has never been repeated.

a dozen women to compete, but Didrikson went by herself. She won five of the eight events she entered: javelin, shot put, 80-meter hurdles, broad jump, and high jump. Didrikson took home the national championship title and qualified for the Olympics.

Although some people were inspired by her athletic ability, many were not. It was rare for women to compete professionally in Didrikson's era. Joe Williams, a sports writer at the New York *Telegraph* newspaper, thought Didrikson didn't belong at the Olympics. "It would be much better if she and her ilk stayed at home, got themselves prettied up, and waited for the phone to ring," he wrote.

Didrikson was not swayed by the disapproval. In the 1932 Olympics, she competed in three events. In the javelin, she broke an Olympic record and claimed the gold medal. In the 80-meter hurdles, she set a new record and grabbed the gold. In the high jump, she came in first but her head cleared the bar a bit before her body. Olympic judges said that method wasn't allowed. They gave Didrikson the silver medal.

Didrikson hurt her shoulder in the Olympics, which prevented her from continuing to compete in track and field. She discovered golf—and loved it—because it challenged her more than any sport ever had. She practiced hour upon hour until she mastered the sport. Didrikson eventually won a total of 82 golf championships. She once won 14 straight tournaments, a record that still stands today. Didrikson also won the Women's Western Open three times. Because there were few opportunities for women in professional golf, she and 12 other women founded the Ladies Professional Golf Association (LPGA).

Babe Didrikson died of cancer at the age of 45. The Associated Press named her the Best Woman Athlete of the Half Century. But Didrikson might have said it in a slightly different way. "The Babe is here," she liked to say. "Who's coming in second?"

Julie Krone
(1963–)
Jockey

At five years old, Julieanne Louise Krone led a horse into the house and asked her mother to saddle it. That same year, she won her first horse show. A decade later, she left home for Louisville, Kentucky, the home of

In 2000, Julie Krone became the first woman inducted into the National Museum of Racing and Hall of Fame. The museum honors the achievements of Thoroughbred racehorses, jockeys, and trainers.

Churchill Downs, the nation's most famous racetrack. She started as a hot walker. Hot walkers lead horses around to cool them down after a race. Her next goal: ride the horse in the race.

For most of horse-racing history, women were just spectators in fancy hats. Krone trampled that idea. She won her first race in 1981, riding Lord Farkle at Tampa Bay Downs. She was the first woman to ride in

the Kentucky Derby. Krone was also the first woman to win a Triple Crown event— the Belmont Stakes. And she was one of a handful of jockeys ever to win six races in a single day.

Along the way, she fell off a few times. Krone broke her ankle, her hands, and her back. A horse once kicked her so hard he literally bruised her heart. But she kept on riding. In her 22-year career as a jockey,

Krone won 3,704 races. At a height of 4 feet 10 inches (147 centimeters), and weight of 100 pounds (45 kilograms), she has sat astride more than 21,000 of the fastest one-ton wonder-horses in the world. In 2019, Krone, who is now retired, started a junior jockey camp to teach riding skills to children during the summer in Cambridge, New York.

Krone has been named to both the Cowgirl Hall of Fame and the National Women's Hall of Fame in Seneca Falls, New York. She was honored with the Wilma Rudolph Courage Award by the National Women's Sports Foundation. But it may be her Belmont Stakes win that matters most to her.

"Over time, I came to appreciate the meaning of my historic ride," Krone said. "Twenty-five years later, girls still come up to me and say, "You inspired me so much. You let me know a girl could do it. That means everything.""

In 1968, Olympic equestrian Kathy Kusner sued the state of Maryland's Gaming Commission and won the right to become a licensed jockey. More than 50 years later, only 8 percent of licensed jockeys in the United States are women.

Diana Taurasi
(1982–)
Scoring Guard, Phoenix Mercury

Diana Taurasi grew up with one foot on grass the other on hardwood, "going from the soccer field to the basketball court, still having my shin guards on. Getting my first new pair of basketball shoes. The burn of the hot asphalt. The *swoosh* of the net and the *whoosh* of the soccer ball through freshly cut grass."

In high school, basketball became her focus. And today, Taurasi is considered by many to be the greatest woman basketball player in the history of the Women's

In 2017, Diana Taurasi (right) became the all-time leading scorer in the Women's National Basketball Association (WNBA).

National Basketball Association (WNBA). She leads the league in points scored: 8,575 points at the end of the 2019 season. She is a four-time Olympic gold-medal winner and three-time WNBA championship winner. Like many players in the WNBA, Taurasi travels overseas during the off-season to play in the EuroLeague, where players can earn as much as 10 times their WNBA salary. Playing for a Russian team, Taurasi has won six EuroLeague championships.

Despite dominating in the WNBA for decades, Taurasi says she still feels like "just a kid from Chino," California, where she grew up.

"I am very much the daughter of immigrants. It's both a point of pride and an essential part of characterizing my upbringing. We spoke Spanish in our house. We listened to Spanish music. All of the TV channels we watched were in Spanish. We ate mostly Italian and Argentinian food. That was my normal; it's all I knew. That's how I understood this country—a myriad of cultures coexisting all at once."

Simone Biles won four Olympic gold medals and one bronze at the 2016 Rio Summer Games, a record in women's gymnastics at a single games.

Simone Biles

(1997–)
Gymnast

When Simone Biles was six, her class was all set to take a field trip to a farm. And then, in what turned out to be a bolt of spectacular good luck, the weather turned bad. So they went to the gym instead. Simone bounced, tumbled, and played— and after watching a gymnast briefly, she did a nearly perfect back handspring. The coaches at Bannon Gymnastix sent home a note inviting her to take classes.

Today, Biles is the most decorated athlete—male or female—in the history of her sport. In August 2019, she showed up at practice for the U.S. Gymnastics Championships wearing a leotard bedazzled with a goat—a visual nod to her status as the "Greatest of All Time."

And Biles isn't afraid to speak proudly about her success. "It's not out of cockiness. I've won five world titles and if I say, 'I'm the best gymnast there is,' [people might say] 'Oh, she's cocky. Look at her now.' No, the facts are literally on the paper."

The numbers back her up: Biles has won 14 world medals—more than any other athlete in the world in any sport. And she continues to create jaw-dropping moves that bear her name. By October 2019, there were four moves called the "Biles." Difficult moves earn more points. By landing them successfully, Biles often wins by a larger margin than any athlete before her. Some of her moves are so complex that the International Gymnastics Federation actually lowered their point value to keep less-experienced athletes from trying them.

Biles is a powerhouse. For one of her floor moves at the 2019 World Championships—a signature "triple-double"—she reportedly jumped 9 feet (274.3 cm) in the air. She rotated twice while turning head over heels three times before landing. She's the only female gymnast in the world who has executed that move.

How Biles got from the mats at Bannon Gymnastix to the pinnacle of her profession is clear. She gave years of her life to the pursuit. Practicing when other kids were playing. Practicing through injury and exhaustion. Practicing, she says, for sheer love of the sport.

Somehow, Simone Biles has managed to keep a quirky, bubbly personality in spite of the relentless hard work of being a professional gymnast.

"I think I'm teaching my teammates that they can still be successful while having fun," she says. That's a signature move that may end up bearing her name someday.

About 30 U.S. gymnasts have had signature moves named for them. That means the gymnast submitted a description of an innovative move and then executed it completely during a major competition.

Chapter 2

GAME CHANGERS: WOMEN IN NEW TERRITORIES

Until the 1970s, sports opportunities for girls and women were limited. At school, boys could choose from many different athletic activities. Girls usually had just a few options. Boys' teams got first claim on the gyms. Boys' teams could hire doctors to treat injuries. They could rent buses to drive them to away games.

Girls were on their own. If they wanted equipment, medical treatment, uniforms, or hotels, they had to get creative, holding bake sales, car washes, or other fundraisers. After college, women's professional sports opportunities were almost nonexistent.

Then came the women's movement. And the civil rights movement. And the push for diversity. Soon women broke all kinds of records—and they kicked down doors that had kept women out of sports.

Keiko Fukuda
(1913–2013)
Judo

It was wartime in Japan. Keiko Fukuda's family—or what was left of it, since the men had been called away to fight in World War II (1939–1945)—built an air-raid shelter where they could hide. They planted potatoes to eat. And despite the danger,

Keiko Fukuda was the last surviving student of Kanō Jigorō, the founder of judo.

30-year-old Keiko Fukuda traveled miles to the Kodokan dojo to teach judo to her students.

Fukuda walked past burning houses. She hid in fields when the B-29 bombers blazed overhead. And she carried with her a nourishing soup to feed her hungry students.

Fukuda's wartime dedication to judo is just one part of a lifetime spent studying and teaching the martial art. She is the only woman ever to reach the tenth dan—the highest level possible in the practice of judo.

When Fukuda began her practice, the traditional Japanese view was that women should marry and raise children, not practice martial arts. Women could only achieve the fifth dan. But when Fukuda received a marriage offer, she turned it down. Judo was her life. Because she pursued judo with such devotion, she opened the path for many other women to study the sport all over the world.

In 1964, when judo was made an official Olympic sport, Keiko Fukuda demonstrated her skills at the Olympic Games in Tokyo, Japan. In 1966, she traveled to the United States and began teaching judo in San Francisco. In 1973, after she became an American citizen, she opened a dojo in honor of her mentor, Kanō Jigorō Shihan, the founder of judo. She taught at her California dojo, and around the world, until she died in 2013 at the age of 99.

Toni Stone
(1921–1996)
Baseball

Toni Stone had a confession to make. The teenager told her family priest she was thinking about running away—so she could join a baseball team. Lucky for her, the priest was open-minded for the 1930s. He found her a spot on the parish boys' team, and *crack!* Her career in baseball took off around the bases.

She had started playing on the sandlots of St. Paul, Minnesota—usually

Toni Stone retired from professional baseball in 1954. In 2019, more than 60 years later, her life story became the basis of a play, Toni Stone.

double-discrimination. She was female, which meant there were few professional sports opportunities. And she was African American, which meant that the only women's professional baseball team wouldn't let her play.

Then came the dream call: The Indianapolis Clowns wanted her to take Hank Aaron's place as second base player when he moved into Major League Baseball. Toni Stone became the first woman to play pro baseball in the Negro League, the league started to give African Americans a chance to play. Her teammates often harassed her, spiking her with the ball and cat-calling her. She held her own against the abuse—even taking a baseball bat to a player who sexually harassed her. But they couldn't argue with her skill.

the only girl among the boys. Then she played on the "barnstorming circuit" before joining a semipro team called the New Orleans Creoles. Even though she played fierce baseball, Toni Stone faced

Stone could run 100 yards in 11 seconds. She had a batting average of .243. And she was one of the few players ever to get a hit off famed pitcher Satchel Paige.

In 1993, the Baseball Hall of Fame recognized Stone along with all the players in the Negro League. Martha Ackmann, author of *Curveball: Toni Stone's Challenge to Baseball and America*, said, "Can you imagine the sight—even today—of a woman playing professional baseball at Yankee Stadium? That's what Stone did."

Janet Guthrie
(1938–)
Auto Racing

When Janet Guthrie attended Miss Harris's Florida School for Girls in Miami, most of her classmates were still being taught that marriage was a woman's best option. But not Janet.

Her father, who was a pilot, taught her to fly airplanes. By 16, she was skydiving. When she graduated college with a degree in physics, she became a pilot herself. Then she realized she could not get a job as a pilot. At that time, women were not hired as commercial or military pilots.

So she bought the sleekest, fastest car she could find: a Jaguar XK 140 Roadster. She worked on the car herself—rebuilding its engine and repairing the body. She started racing it in the Sports Car Club of America, where women had been allowed to race for decades. She built a winning record over a period of 13 years. An auto designer and owner named Rolla Vollstedt asked her to race his car in the Indianapolis 500—a race no woman had ever entered before. In May 1979, the Indianapolis Motor Speedway president made a famous announcement: "In company with the first lady ever to qualify for the Indianapolis 500—gentlemen, start your engines."

Janet Guthrie remembers, "Coming out of turn 4 on the final lap of my qualifying run, I could see Rolla and the guys on the crew leaping and waving their arms. I'm

Janet Guthrie in front of her car at the Daytona International Speedway on February 20, 1977.

not sure whether the lump at the back of my throat was actually my heart, but I am utterly certain that I didn't breathe until the yard of bricks at the start/finish rolled under my wheels and the checkered flag swirled overhead."

Not long after that, she crossed another finish line: Guthrie became the first woman to race in the NASCAR Daytona 500. Overall, Janet Guthrie raced in 33 NASCAR events and 11 IndyCar events. She was inducted into the International Hall of Motorsports Fame in 2006.

In 2019, Jamie Chadwick of England won the first all-women W series motorsports race, taking home the $500,000 prize. The race is intended to help women break into Formula One racing. Only one woman has ever scored in a Formula One race—Italian Lella Lombardi in 1975.

Alana Nichols

(1983–)

Wheelchair Basketball/Adaptive Alpine Skiing/Paracanoe/Adaptive Surfing

Alana Nichols drops down the face of the wave, digging her paddle into the swell. At this moment, she is all athlete. Focused. Driven. Loving the challenge thrown at her by "Mama Ocean."

"I know she's not out to hurt me," Nichols said, speaking about the sea, "but she's powerful enough to end my life."

To her, the ocean is a kind of healer. The big blue was there for her, she says, when she needed it most.

Nichols competes in adaptive sports—athletic events where the equipment has been adapted to enable athletes with disabilities to compete. When Nichols was 17, she tried to do a backflip while snowboarding. She landed on a rock. A tingling wave surged down her back, and then her legs went numb. That accident left her partially paralyzed.

At first, she was plunged into shock and grief. She had been an athlete all her life—competing was part of her identity. The months after the accident were a dark time. Then one day, coming out of a physical

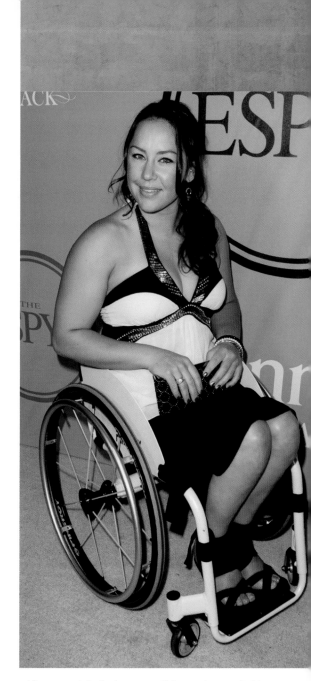

Along with being an Olympic medalist and ESPY award winner, Alana Nichols gives motivational talks and supports a wide variety of charities.

therapy session, she passed a gym full of people playing wheelchair basketball. It looked rough. The ball moved fast. The wheelchairs clanged off each other. Nichols decided to give it a try—and within a year she was competing internationally. In 2008, she and her teammates won gold during the Paralympic Games in Beijing, China.

From there, she took on Alpine skiing, becoming the only woman to win gold at both the summer and winter Paralympics. Then came another accident. While Alpine skiing in the Sochi Olympic Games, she struck a rock, broke both her ankles, and tore three ligaments in her shoulder.

That's why she found her way into the water. It was a more forgiving surface than boulder-studded trails. Now, with six medals in three sports and two world championship titles in adaptive surfing, Nichols remembers the sadness she felt after her first injury.

"I thought back to that 17-year old girl that couldn't imagine living her life in a wheelchair and who thought her athletic life was over," Nichols told an interviewer. "Little did I know it was just beginning, and that it was going to be bigger and better than I had ever imagined."

PEDAL-PUSHERS—HOW BIKE RIDING HELPED WOMEN WIN THE VOTE

It might surprise you to learn that a piece of sports equipment helped win women the right to vote. In the late 1800s and early 1900s, a new kind of bicycle allowed ordinary women to get outdoors, get healthy exercise, and even get to meetings about the vote. Many women stopped wearing binding clothes like petticoats and corsets so they could pedal their bikes freely. As women got stronger physically, they got stronger politically too. By 1920, these pedal-pushing, protest-marching women had won the right to vote in American elections.

Chapter 3

INTO THE BLUE: WOMEN ATHLETES IN THE SEA AND SKY

The Greek and Roman pantheon is full of sea and sky goddesses. They controlled winds and waves. They granted safe passage to sailors. They made tides rise and irrigated fertile floodplains. Just like the goddesses, the women in this chapter exercised amazing powers both in the air and in the water.

Tiny Broadwick
(1893–1978)
Skydiving

There are birds with wingspans longer than Georgia Ann Thompson's whole body. She stood 5 feet (152.4 cm) tall and weighed just 80 pounds (36.3 kg)—hence her nickname "Tiny." Condensed in her small frame, however, was a vast quantity of courage.

At the age of 15, Tiny jumped out of a flying hot air balloon, released her parachute, and drifted down toward the 1908 North Carolina State Fair, where shocked spectators watched in amazement. "I tell you," she said later, "it was the most wonderful sensation in the world."

To get the parachute job, Thompson approached a man named Charles

Tiny Broadwick with her parachute pack next to an airplane, September 17, 1920.

Broadwick, who managed a troupe called "The Broadwicks and their Famous French Aeronauts." Eventually, Broadwick began touring the nation with the performers. Charles legally adopted her.

During her career, she faced danger many times. Once she landed on top of a moving train. Another time she fell into a windmill's blades. Once she got tangled in electrical wires. Sometimes she even broke bones when she landed. None of that deterred her.

In 1913, she became the first woman ever to parachute from an airplane. The plane, piloted by Glen Martin, climbed to an altitude of 2,000 feet (610 meters). Then Broadwick pulled a lever that dropped her seat out from under her. Her parachute instantly deployed and she drifted down to safety in Griffith Park in Los Angeles, California.

In 1914, Broadwick became the first woman to parachute from a hydroplane into Lake Michigan. She went on to make more than 1,100 aerial jumps. When the U.S. Army needed to demonstrate parachute technology to soldiers, they called on Tiny Broadwick to show them how it worked.

This petite daredevil was inducted into the Early Birds, an organization made up of aeronautical pioneers. In 1964, one of Broadwick's parachutes was donated to the Smithsonian National Air and Space Museum in honor of her sky-high achievements.

Gertrude Ederle
(1905–2003)
Swimming

"She's drowning!" someone cried.

It had been several minutes since anyone saw Gertrude Ederle move, and in a moment of panic, a crew member reached into the chill waters of the English Channel to grab her. That touch instantly disqualified Ederle, who was not drowning—just resting—during the long

35-mile (56.3 km) channel swim. Ederle was not pleased.

The next year, 1926, Ederle tried again. Swimming the English Channel takes intense preparation. Rough seas, strong tides, and cold water make this one of the toughest open-water feats in the world.

Ederle smeared herself with sheep grease to keep warm. She donned a two-piece swimsuit she had designed to reduce the water's drag. And she entered the turbulent channel that separates France from England.

Ederle prayed.

She sang to keep her stroke regular.

She refused to give up even when rain fell and the waves reportedly grew to 20-foot (6 m) heights. Fourteen hours and 31 minutes after she set off, she waded onto an English beach. Gertrude Ederle was the first woman ever to swim the English Channel—and she did it faster than anyone, male or female, had ever done before.

Though Ederle had already won one gold and two bronze medals in the 1924 Paris Olympics and set women's

Gertrude Ederle was the first woman to swim across the English Channel.

freestyle swimming records in her swimming career, the channel swim would remain her most famous accomplishment.

When she returned home to New York City, more than two million fans greeted her in a ticker-tape parade. She traveled the country, attracting huge crowds, and in the years after her channel swim, there was a dramatic spike in the number of women earning Red Cross swimming certificates. After her retirement, Ederle spent her time teaching deaf children how to swim.

Georgie White
(1911–1992)
White Water Rafting

Georgie White at Grand Canyon National Park, 1957

There's a spirited stretch of rapids in the Colorado River known as the "roaring twenties," where the water bucks up green and white peaks among the red rocks of the Grand Canyon.

The rapids at Mile 24 are named "Georgie," after Georgie White, the first woman to run a commercial river rafting company in the Grand Canyon.

Her first encounter with the river was not in a boat at all. Reeling from grief following the death of her daughter in a biking accident, White swam a 60-mile (96.5 km) course of the river with a friend over four days. They were equipped only with swimsuits and backpacks. They ate powdered candy, powdered coffee, and powdered soup.

After that journey, she was hooked. She and her friend Henry Alesworth bought inflatable Army rescue rafts, lashed them together for safety, and started guiding tourists down the river. She called the company Royal River Rats. The trips were cheap—just $300 for a 10-day run. At the time, companies run by men charged around three times as much.

Georgie White kept running the Colorado River until she was 80 years old. During her career, she guided more than 12,000 people through one of the most life-changing landscapes in wild America.

Jill Heinerth is considered one of the world's best cave divers.

Jill Heinerth
(1965–)
Cave Diver

In February 2001—the peak of summer in Antarctica—Jill Heinerth and her guide raced across the sea ice on a snowmobile.

They sped because the iceberg that had broken free from the Ross Ice Shelf would soon drift out to sea and dissolve. They sped because as climate change melts glaciers and raises sea levels, Heinerth wanted to document the drastic changes in the world's ice caps—by photographing them from deep inside.

As she descended into the icy depths of the glacier's caves, Heinerth practiced thinking like both a diver and a scientist. She noted the layers that showed the iceberg was thousands of years in the making. She photographed streamers of algae stuck to the underside of the ice—algae that would nourish the phytoplankton and zooplankton other sea creatures feed on. This is her life's work: exploring, filming, and photographing the world's underwater caves.

Jill Heinerth has logged more than 7,000 dives in her career, in cave systems from the Yucatán in Mexico to iceberg caves in Antarctica. In 1999, she set a world record for an underwater cave dive when she swam 10,000 feet (3,048 m) at a depth of 310 feet (94.5 m) in Wakulla Springs, Florida.

The work is risky, and Heinerth knows nearly 100 divers who have died underwater. She takes the risk every day, not just because of the extreme beauty of the watery catacombs of the earth, and not just because diving is an extreme physical challenge.

> *For me, it was so worth it to have that experience, to document a place that maybe no one will ever see again.*
> —Jill Heinerth

HAENYEO—KOREAN DEEP SEA DIVERS

Off the tip of South Korea lies an island surrounded by harsh, cold seas. The icy waters around Jeju are home to a rich variety of marine life. Jeju is also home to some of the world's bravest divers. For generations, *haenyeo* (which means *sea women*) have descended into the deep using only wet suits and flippers—no breathing gear—so they can harvest seafood to support their families. As often as 100 times a day, they dive 20 to 40 feet (6 to 12 m) to find abalone, oysters, and other shellfish. When they rise to the surface, they exhale with a special whistle called *sumbi-sori*.

It's a dangerous job. Every year, divers perish in the sea. In recent years, the number of haenyeo has been dropping because Jeju is becoming a popular vacation spot. Some experts believe this generation of haenyeo may be the last.

Chapter 4

RABBLE-ROUSERS: ATHLETES FOR SOCIAL JUSTICE

Many people don't think athletes should speak out about politics or social issues. But in the United States, there is a long, proud tradition of athletes using the power of their platform to speak out for social justice. Here are just a few of the women who have raised their voices to change the world they live in.

Wyomia Tyus
(1945–)
Track and Field

Wyomia Tyus describes her childhood as a safe haven. Beyond the farm where she lived in Griffin, Georgia, segregation and Jim Crow made life harsh and dangerous for African Americans. But on the farm, she and her three brothers ran through the fields and woods, fished in ponds stocked with bass and bream, and ate blackberries through the long Georgia summers.

She was tough—if someone called her or her brothers a racist name, Wyomia taught that person a quick lesson with her fists. Like most girls of the era, she got dolls for Christmas, but she and her brothers used them as footballs.

"They could knock me down 20 times,

Wyomia Tyus during the award ceremony in the 1968 Summer Olympics in Mexico City, Mexico.

and I'd be back up fighting. 'Could you just stay down?' they would say. But I never would," she said.

But when Tyus was 14, a fire destroyed her house, and a year later her beloved father passed away. That double loss knocked her down hard. She barely spoke. She felt utterly lost. It was running that helped her, in time, get back up again.

Ed Temple, coach of the Tennessee State University track team, spotted Tyus's talent and recruited her. She struggled with college studies at first, but Temple expected excellence in studies as well as sports. Tyus studied hard and trained hard, and by 1964, she had made the U.S. Olympic team. Tyus broke the world record and won a gold medal in the 100-meter sprint. In 1968, Tyus graduated from Tennessee State. In the Olympic Games that year, Tyus won another gold in the 100-meter event. No person in history had ever won two back-to-back gold medals in the 100-meter.

During those games, Tyus wore black

SKATEISTAN

In Kabul, Afghanistan, hidden behind high walls, is a school where girls can learn to read, write—and skateboard. In 2008, Australian skateboarder Oliver Percovich started Skateistan, a non-profit organization that builds community in places like Afghanistan and Cambodia, where schools don't always have the funds for sports programs. In Afghanistan, girls are not encouraged to play sports or go to school. The good news is that in Afghanistan, skateboarding isn't considered a sport. Today, Afghanistan has the largest percentage of female skateboarders in the world. In 2020, a film about the school, called *Learning to Skateboard in a War Zone (If You're a Girl)* won an Oscar for Best Documentary (Short Subject).

shorts instead of white ones to signal her support for the civil rights movement. She and her teammates dedicated their medals to runners Tommie Smith and John Carlos. Smith and Carlos had won gold and bronze medals. But they were expelled from the games after they raised their fists in protest at the medal ceremony.

Tyus's protest was not reported at the time. Today, it stands as part of a long tradition of civil rights protests in the United States.

Renée Richards
(1934–)
Tennis

Renée Richards stood in the hotel gift shop, stunned to see a book titled *Man into Woman*, about a Dutch painter who transitioned from male to female. At the time, Richards was just a teenager in town to compete in a tennis tournament. Books like this one were very rare in the late 1940s. Its subject was already familiar to Richards,

Renée Richards in action during the 1979 U.S. Open in Flushing, New York.

whose body and gender identity did not match—but many years would pass before Richards would transition.

"It was a very quiet secret if somebody wanted to have a sex change," Richards says. "You did it quietly and started a new life—frequently in a new city with a new name, and total change of identity."

Eventually, Richards did have surgery. Afterward, she moved to California and began a kind of second life. A Yale-trained eye surgeon, she opened a private practice and began seeing patients. Richards also kept playing tennis. Through college and medical school, from one coast to another, though many aspects of Richards' life changed, tennis was a constant. Captain of the Yale tennis team, Richards had qualified for the U.S. Open five times before the transition.

Then in 1976, Richards won a tournament that would have qualified her for the U.S. Open again—but this time, a reporter outed her after a spectator recognized Richards' unique serve. There was a huge outcry. The national tennis associations and the U.S. Open Committee said any player who wanted to compete professionally had to take a medical test to prove that she was genetically a woman.

Richards sued. The case went all the way to the New York State Supreme Court, and Richards won. It was an important ruling for transgender athletes in all sports. In 2000, Renée Richards was inducted into the U.S. Tennis Association East Hall of Fame.

In 2019, Richards told a reporter, "My biggest achievements are as an eye surgeon—I've operated on more than 20,000 children's eyes. But my legacy is probably going to be more my career in human rights. I never really did much actively. I just did something that served as an example."

Ibtihaj Muhammad
(1985–)
Fencing

Ibtihaj Muhammad excelled in sports. In middle school, she played basketball and volleyball—but team uniforms often conflicted with the principles of her faith. Muhammad is Muslim, and she is committed to modest dress. To play in most sports, she had to put on extra layers to cover her arms and legs.

Then one day when she was still in middle school, she and her mother caught a glimpse of some girls fencing. Long sleeves. Long pants. A mask that covered the same area a hijab would cover. That's how the multitalented athlete found her sport.

"Once I had my uniform on and my mask went on," she said, "people didn't see me for my race. They didn't see me for my religion. They didn't see me for my gender."

Very often, her opponents just saw her as the winner. Muhammad practices fencing with the same intellectual

In 2017, Dr. Muslimah Ali Najee-ullah led a 12-woman, all-Muslim team in the Ragnar Relay, a 200-mile (322-kilometer) relay race.

Ibtihaj Muhammad celebrated her victory in the Women's Individual Sabre event during the 2016 Olympic Games in Rio de Janeiro, Brazil.

power she brings to her schoolwork and the same dedication she gives to her faith. That combination of talent and determination took her all the way to the Olympics.

In 2016, Muhammad became the first African American, Muslim American woman to compete in the Olympics while wearing a hijab. She took home an Olympic medal. In 2019, Mattel announced the first Barbie to wear a hijab—in honor of Ibtihaj Muhammad.

In her memoir, she writes: "As we marched into Rio's Maracanã Stadium that evening, I ended up walking in the front line only a few feet away from Michael Phelps and the American flag," she says. "Dressed in my white pants, navy-blue blazer, and white hijab, waving to the cheering crowds, knowing that more than three billion people were watching all over the world, I truly felt all parts of my identity were being applauded."

ASIJA—HIJABS (FOR THE WIN)

When Fatimah Hussein began coaching Muslim girls who wanted to play basketball, she discovered that Muslim girls were willing to play in girl-only gyms but not on school sports teams. Many girls weren't comfortable with team uniforms. She also saw that after an hour of play, hijabs would be falling off, which distracted players. In 2017, Hussein founded Asija, a sports hijab company that creates head coverings for athletes. Later that year, Nike, too, made headlines by selling its pro hijab. Asija and Nike are responding to the rising number of Muslim girls and women who want to play sports.

The U.S. Women's National Soccer Team after winning the 2019 FIFA Women's World Cup.

The U.S. Women's National Soccer Team

Soccer

In the final match of the 2019 FIFA Women's World Cup in Lyon, France, 58,000 fans shook the Parc Olympique Lyonnais stadium with their cheers. They groaned at missed goals and whooped when the ball found the net. But they were also chanting something you don't hear at most World Cup finals.

"Equal pay!" the fans cried. "Equal pay!"

Down on the pitch, the members of the 2019 U.S. Women's National Soccer Team (USWNT) knew they were playing for more than a trophy—as extraordinary as that trophy is. Just months before the World Cup competition began, the team filed a lawsuit against the U.S. Soccer Federation. They were fighting back against years of unequal treatment.

For the entire history of women's international soccer, women players have been paid less than male players. Exactly how much less depends on the game. For regular season games, the women earn around 89 percent of the salary for male players. For winning the Women's World Cup, the champs earned $4 million—while in 2018 the winners of the Men's World Cup won $38 million.

The women's team also brings in more money than the men's team. Between 2016 and 2018, USWNT games brought in $900,000 more than the men's team. Women players are often made to play under more dangerous conditions too.

The 2019 U.S. Women's National Soccer Team triumphed in Lyons' stadium, making it the fourth time the team has won the Women's World Cup. But their battle isn't over yet. They've got a tough new goal in front of them—making sure a jury is the next group of fans to stand up for equal pay.

> *We show up for a game. If we win the game, if we lose the game, if we tie the game, we want to be paid equally, period.*
> —Megan Rapinoe, team captain

EUNICE KENNEDY SHRIVER AND THE SPECIAL OLYMPICS

Eunice Kennedy, sister of U.S. President John F. Kennedy, remembers how much fun it was to sail with her sister Rosemary. Rosemary had an intellectual disability.

"I would take her as a crew in our boat races. . . . She was especially helpful with the jib and she loved to be in the winning boat. Winning at anything always brought a marvelous smile to her face," Eunice said in 1962.

To celebrate her sister's love for sports, Eunice Kennedy started a summer camp that offered sports to children with intellectual disabilities. It was wildly successful. The camp grew. In 1968, the first Special Olympics Games opened in Chicago. Today, more than 7,000 athletes from all over the world compete in 26 summer sporting events. The winter games draw 3,000 international athletes.

Chapter 5

SIDELINES: WOMEN REFEREES, COACHES, AND ANNOUNCERS

It takes more than great players to make great sports possible. Coaches teach players, driving them to better performance. Announcers call games as they happen, making viewers feel in-the-stadium excitement. And referees hold players accountable, keeping things fair in the heat of the game.

By January 2020, Major League Baseball (MLB), the National Hockey League (NHL), the National Football League (NFL), and the National Basketball Association (NBA) had women coaches on staff.

Violet Palmer
(1964–)
National Basketball Association (NBA) Official

Violet Palmer grew up in Compton, California—the daughter of strict Baptist parents who held her to high standards. "As long as you got good grades in my house you could do whatever you wanted," said Palmer.

Violet Palmer officiated 54 NBA games during her first season. She would work as an NBA official for 18 seasons before her retirement in 2016.

And what she wanted was basketball.

She played in high school and college, helping her team win two NCAA Division II women's national championships.

"My student-athlete experience taught me those essential things in life, not only as a basketball player but as a human being. It was dedication. It was hard work. It was the work ethic every single day," she says.

But after college, Palmer had to find another career path. She could not play professional basketball because the WNBA did not exist when she graduated in 1986. So she trained as a referee, donned a striped shirt, and began officiating. From the first whistle blow, she knew she'd found something special. And in the end, she came to love the sport of officiating even more than she loved basketball.

Then, in 1997, her phone rang. It was the NBA. Violet Palmer became the first woman to officiate a professional sporting event.

"I was scared out of my wits," she remembers. "I felt like the entire world was expecting me to fail. But as soon as I walked out on that court and the ball went up, it all went away. I was just a referee refereeing another basketball game."

At first, some people fought the idea of a woman referee. They said things like, "Go back to the kitchen." But Palmer focused on doing her job well, and pretty soon the haters hushed. In 2014, Palmer made history again when she married her girlfriend of 20 years. She became the first openly gay referee in the NBA.

At the time of her retirement in 2016, Violet Palmer had officiated at 919 games. Today, she is helping the NBA train a new generation of referees.

Jill Ellis

(1966–)

U.S. Women's National Soccer Team Coach

Her passion for soccer came from England, where Jill Ellis spent her childhood years cheering for Manchester

Jill Ellis was the first coach to win back-to-back World Cup titles, in 2015 and 2019.

1970s, girls did not play soccer in England; it was a sport for boys. It was the United States that let her onto the pitch.

When Jill Ellis was 14, her father, a soccer coach, moved the family to Virginia so he could start a soccer academy there. That meant Jill would have a chance to play on a team. She joined the Braddock Road Bluebells, and in short order, they won the first Under-19 (U19) U.S. Youth Soccer National Championship. In 1984, her high school team won the State Championship in Virginia.

After college at William & Mary, Jill started a corporate job that left her feeling trapped in a cubicle. So she left the solid earnings behind and became an assistant soccer coach, first at University of Maryland and then at the University of California, Los Angeles, where she took her teams to eight NCAA championships.

United. "I remember kicking a tennis ball around the backyard with my brother, with flower pots as goalposts, and joining in with the boys in the schoolyard," she said.

But England could not give her a chance to play the game she loved. In the

Jill Ellis went on to coach the U.S. Women's National Soccer Team (USWNT) to two consecutive Women's World Cup victories. She is the most successful coach in the team's history—having guided them to 101 wins and only seven losses.

She humbly credits her dad when she talks about her record, recalling his talent with the athletes he coached. "He had the ability to connect with them all, to make the game interesting and fun, and engage them in what he was doing. I was in awe of that," she says. "It stuck with me—taught me early on that it is about connecting with players, no matter what their age."

Lesley Visser
(1953–)
Sportscaster

Lesley Visser remembers the words of wisdom her mother spoke when she said she wanted to grow up to be a sports writer: "Sometimes you have to cross

In 2017, Lesley Visser was inducted into the Sports Broadcasting Hall of Fame.

when the sign says don't walk."

She took her mother's advice and crossed into territory few women occupied. She started out as a sports writer for *The Boston Globe* in an era when women weren't even allowed on the field or in the press boxes. Her first press badge read, "No women and children allowed." She had to hijack players in parking lots to snatch a quick interview.

Slowly, the world of sports broadcasting opened new opportunities for women, and Visser's grasp of sports and her skill as a journalist led to a 40-year career. In an era when female sportscasters were often viewed as "eye candy," Visser was seen as a top-notch sportswriter who just happened to look good on TV.

Visser was the first woman inducted into the NFL Hall of Fame. Voted the number one female sports announcer of all time, she is the only person to have covered the Final Four, NBA Finals, the World Series, the Triple Crown, Monday Night Football, the Super Bowl, the Olympics, the World Figure Skating Championships, and the U.S. Open tennis tournament.

Sarah Thomas
(1973–)
National Football League (NFL) Official

If you watch the video, you can see the hit coming. Green Bay safety Morgan Burnett tackles Minnesota Vikings tight end Kyle Rudolph—and takes down line judge Sarah Thomas too. Thomas, the first woman official in the NFL, stepped off the field briefly to be checked for a concussion. Within minutes, she was back. She continued blowing the whistle for the rest of the game even though her wrist was broken.

Thomas knows a thing or two about tough sports. Throughout high school and college she played softball and basketball. At the time, she told reporters she hated referees. But when she was looking for a

In 2015, Sarah Thomas became the first permanent female official in the NFL.

way to keep active in sports later in her life, her brother mentioned becoming a football referee. "Can girls do that?" she asked.

Thomas trained hard, then refereed for high school football games for 10 years. She moved up to college football and put in another eight years. She became the first woman to officiate a major college football game, the first to officiate in a Big Ten stadium, and the first to officiate a bowl game.

By then, even the NFL could see that the answer to Thomas's question is *yes*. Girls *can* do that.

In 2015, Sarah Thomas became the first woman to call professional football games in the NFL. In 2019, she became the first woman to officiate in an NFL playoff game. Her whistle and flag are on display in the NFL Hall of Fame.

EVERYDAY HEROES

In 1972, 90 percent of women's college sports teams were coached by women. By 2014, that number had dropped to 43 percent. In youth sports, the number is even lower: just 27 percent.

When girls have women coaches, they see what it looks like when women lead. They hear women speak with authority. They are coached by people who understand their bodies, their sport, and their drive to win.

Brittney Burgess, who played basketball and volleyball in college and was a two-time track and field All-American, knew she wanted a career in coaching.

"Becoming a coach was a no-brainer for me," Burgess says. "I knew exactly the type of coach I wanted to be . . . someone athletes could trust, depend on, and learn from as they grow on the court and off the court." Research shows that when girls have positive coaches—like Burgess and thousands of other women—they stay in sports longer.

The University of Minnesota has been studying coaching in women's collegiate sports. They track statistics across 86 different colleges. Their 2018-2019 study found that the number of women coaches continues to increase.

→ In 2012–2013, the study's first year, 40.2% of coaches were women.

→ By the 2018–2019 season, it was up to 41.8%.

→ Some sports have a higher percentage. Nearly 96% of field hockey teams, 83% of lacrosse teams, and 75% of equestrian teams are coached by women.

→ Basketball and gymnastics are on the higher end, with around 60% female-led teams.

→ Nordic skiing, rifle, and tennis are about even between men and women.

→ Volleyball, hockey, soccer, track, swimming and diving, and rowing are some of the sports on the lower end.

→ Other sports have a ways to go. Alpine skiing and triathlon had no female coaches.

Chapter 6

ALL FOR ONE, ONE FOR ALL: TRIUMPHANT TEAMS

In her book *Wolfpack: How to Come Together, Unleash Our Power, and Change the Game*, Abby Wambach talks about the biggest lesson she learned as captain of the U.S. Women's National Soccer Team. She learned not to believe in the word *impossible*. Wambach writes, "A team of women who unites for a larger goal can achieve the impossible again and again."

These teams know all about defying the word *impossible*. They have made their names known as some of the most daring, victorious teams in sports history.

All-American Girls Professional Baseball League
Baseball

In 1941, the United States entered World War II. Many baseball players were among those sent to fight—so America's pastime was paused. But not for long. The All-American Girls Professional Baseball League (AAGPBL) was formed in 1943. Professional scouts traveled the United States and Canada in search of the best athletes. Of the hundreds who tried out, just

The AAGPBL gave more than 600 women a chance to play pro baseball.

60 players made the cut. At first, the public thought the league was silly: Girls playing professional ball? No way.

Little by little, however, the stands filled up. In 1944, when the league featured six teams, about 259,000 people showed up to see the women play. By 1946, attendance ballooned to 754,000 fans in the stands. Games attracted just as many men as they did women.

Even though the women played pro ball, team managers made them take "charm" classes and wear short dresses to please the crowds. After the war ended and male players returned to the field, crowds at the women's games slowly dwindled. The last teams disbanded in 1954.

The 1976 Yale Women's Rowing Crew
Rowing

In Connecticut, February and March are cold. Really cold. If you've just finished a rowing competition in a freezing river, you want a warm shower and dry clothes. In 1976, if you were a member of the all-male Yale Rowing Club, that's what you got. But not if you were a member of the Yale Women's Rowing Club. There were no facilities for women in the boathouse.

Ginny Gilder, a member of the Yale Women's Rowing Team, said, "Fifteen to twenty minutes after the women got on the bus, sweaty, soaked, and by now, often shivery, the men would straggle on, clean, hair freshly combed, wrapped in warm jackets, and eager to hit the dining hall for dinner." The women's team just had to shiver it out.

"No matter the weather," Ginny recalls, "we waited for the men in wet clothes, we ate our meals in wet clothes, and we walked back to our dorm rooms in wet clothes."

But one March day, they'd had enough. They stripped down, totally naked, in the office of their coach. They had painted "Title IX" on their chests and backs. The team captain read from a statement, saying,

The Yale Women's Rowing Club won the Eastern Sprints and the National Championship in 1979. Many of the 1976 rowers were core members of that team.

"These are the bodies Yale is exploiting. We have come here today to make clear how unprotected we are."

Their bold action got them the attention they needed. A year later, Yale finally put a women's locker room in the boathouse.

What Is Title IX?

Title IX is the section of the Civil Rights Act of 1964 that protects people in schools from discrimination based on their sex. It says, "No person in the United States shall, on the basis of sex, be excluded from participation in, be denied the benefits of, or be subjected to discrimination under any education program or activity receiving Federal financial assistance." That means if a school gets money from the federal government, they have to treat athletes equally.

Tracy Edwards (third from left, front) and the crew of the Maiden *after completing the Whitbread Round the World Race.*

Tracy Edwards

(1962–)
and the Crew of the *Maiden*
Sailing

"You're all going to die."

This was the message Tracy Edwards heard when she announced that her all-women crew was going to sail around the world in the 1989 Whitbread Round the World Race. No female crew had attempted the race before. Sailing was considered a man's sport. But Edwards and her crew defied the attitudes of the day. They bought a broken boat, stripped it down, and rebuilt it. They found sponsors to help pay for the expensive journey.

They set sail from Southampton, England, on September 2, 1989, and sailed to Punta del Este, Uruguay. From there, they sailed through the southern sea, tossed on 50-foot (15-m) waves, surrounded by icebergs, to reach Fremantle, Australia. They came in first in their class in this leg. They also won the next leg, from Fremantle to Auckland, New Zealand. Facing 100 days with no wind and a dangerous leak in open waters, they lost their lead in the next leg, which finished in Fort Lauderdale, Florida. On May 28, 1990, *Maiden* finished the race, coming in second overall in her class. They were the first all-women crew to race the Whitbread.

> *Define your own course and keep moving forward. You will absolutely end up where you need to be.*
> —Tracy Edwards

The Whitbread Round the World Race began in 1973. It takes place every three years. To get around the world, boats of many different sizes sail six short trips called "legs," totaling 32,000 miles (51,500 km).

Misty May-Treanor
(1977–) and
Kerri Walsh Jennings
(1978–)
Beach Volleyball

Before the 2012 London Olympics, teammates Misty May-Treanor and Kerri Walsh Jennings watched a video they had created to charge themselves up. Patched in among clips of family and inspiring quotes, there were *lions*. Roaring, slashing lions defending what was theirs. May-Treanor and Jennings had quite a lot to defend in London.

Misty May-Treanor (left) and Kerri Walsh Jennings first teamed up in 2001. May-Traenor retired from beach volleyball after the London Olympics in 2012.

They were two-time Olympic gold medal winners and widely considered the best beach volleyball team of all time. They had built a sporting relationship defined by winning, going 112 matches in a row without a single defeat. The lions in the video reminded them of who they were in the game: hunters.

At the London Olympics, the pair defeated another top American duo, April Ross and Jennifer Kessey, to win the gold for an unprecedented third time.

Both Jennings and May-Treanor describe their team as "magical." But it didn't necessarily start out that way. They already knew each other from playing indoor volleyball—both players excelled in high school and college. But Walsh Jennings wasn't interested in taking the sport to the beach at first.

"I don't play beach volleyball because I don't want to look like an idiot in the sand," she said at the time.

Then, she gave the sport a shot. At the suggestion of their mothers, the two young women began forging a team. It turns out that to make magic in beach volleyball, what you need is equal parts sand, sweat, and time, plus the roar of lions who are not going to let any living thing take away what they know belongs to them.

Grand Slam champions Serena Williams (left) and Venus Williams at the 2013 U.S. Open in New York.

Venus Williams

(1980–) and

Serena Williams

(1981–)

Tennis

Has there ever been a better team than this one? As a tennis duo, they are a powerhouse: 22 doubles titles, 3 Olympic gold medals, and 14 Grand Slam tournaments. That's in addition to the titles and medals they have accrued as individuals. These women are devoted to playing the game—and winning.

They are also devoted to each other. Even when they face off against one another, as they have done in more than 30 tournaments, they do not utter a critical word to the press. No matter who wins the game, set, and match, family comes in first.

"Playing Venus is like playing myself," Serena says, "because we grew up playing together, we grew up practicing together. It's something that's been difficult because she has been my toughest opponent."

In early interviews, when they were still young enough to have been squabbling siblings, they deferred to each other and praised each other publicly. Serena confessed to Oprah Winfrey that until she was 18 years old, she copied everything Venus did—right down to ordering the same food.

These athlete-sisters grew up in the public eye. They began training at the age of 3, supervised by their father, and both girls began competing professionally at the age of 14. They faced racial prejudice and gender bias. They have endured family tragedies. They have helped each other over health-related hurdles—in addition to building the most astonishing collection of titles and trophies in the world. Yet what makes the Williams sisters the GOAT (Greatest of All Time) is something more than just the number in the "Win" column. It's the wins plus the love.

"In my life, it's always going to be Venus and Serena," younger sister Serena said. "On the court we are mortal enemies. But the second we shake hands we are best friends again."

Every girl, every woman, has the power within her to become an athlete. If you are already running, dribbling, shooting, swimming, dancing—keep going. If you are not yet on the track or in the pool, you can start looking for your sport today. The women in this book have cleared a path for you. So go, girl!

WOMEN ATHLETES IN ANCIENT GREECE

Women did not compete in the Olympic Games in ancient Greece. Married women were not even allowed to watch the games—perhaps because male athletes competed in the nude. But there is some early archaeological evidence that shows women had their own games. Sometime around 700 BC, a festival in honor of Hera, the wife of Zeus, was started. The festival was held every four years. It included foot races and races in which women wore armor and drove chariots.

FEMALE PARTICIPATION AT THE
WINTER OLYMPIC GAMES

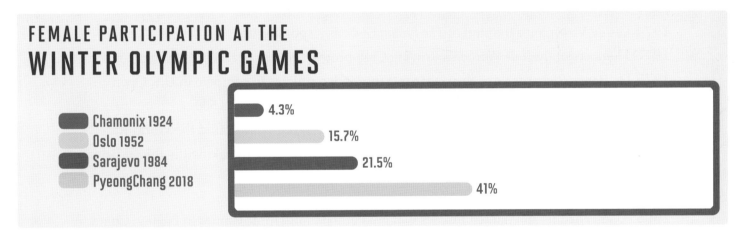

Chamonix 1924 — 4.3%
Oslo 1952 — 15.7%
Sarajevo 1984 — 21.5%
PyeongChang 2018 — 41%

FEMALE PARTICIPATION AT THE
SUMMER OLYMPIC GAMES

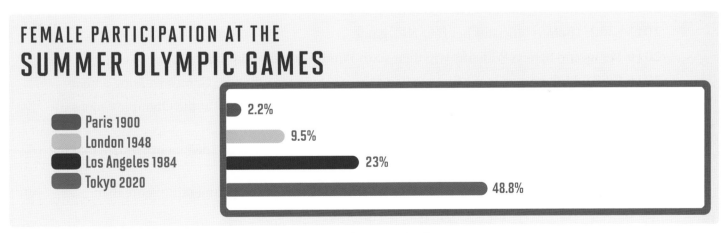

Paris 1900 — 2.2%
London 1948 — 9.5%
Los Angeles 1984 — 23%
Tokyo 2020 — 48.8%

Since 1991, the International Olympic Committee has required any new Olympic sport to include women's events.

Timeline

1913 Tiny Broadwick becomes the first woman ever to parachute from an airplane.

1926 Gertrude Ederle swims across the English Channel.

1932 Babe Didrikson Zaharias wins two Olympic gold medals.

1944 The All-American Girls Professional Baseball League (AAGPBL) opens.

1945 Georgie White and a friend swim a 60-mile (96.5 km) stretch of the Colorado River.

1953 Toni Stone becomes the first woman to play baseball in the Negro League.

1964 Title IX of the Civil Rights Act makes equal opportunity for all student athletes the law.

1966 Keiko Fukuda begins teaching judo in the United States.

1968 Wyomia Tyus wins an Olympic gold medal in the 100-meter sprint and dedicates her win to Tommie Smith and John Carlos, two black athletes banned from the games for their civil rights protest.

1968 With Eunice Kennedy Shriver's support, the first Special Olympic Games opens in Chicago.

1974 Lesley Visser joins the staff of *The Boston Globe* as a sportswriter.

1976 Members of the Yale Women's Rowing Club protest the lack of facilities for women athletes.

1977 Dr. Renée Richards wins the right for transgender athletes to compete in U.S. Open.

1979 Janet Guthrie becomes the first woman to race in the Indianapolis 500.

1990 Tracy Edwards and the crew of the *Maiden* win the Whitbread Round the World Race.

1993 Julie Krone becomes first woman to win a Triple Crown race by taking the title at Belmont Stakes on a horse named Colonial Affair.

1997 Violet Palmer referees her first NBA game.

2008 Alana Nichols and her teammates win gold at the Paralympic Games in Beijing, China.

2012 Misty May-Treanor and Kerri Walsh Jennings win their third Olympic gold medal.

2015 Sarah Thomas officiates her first NFL game.

2016 Venus and Serena Williams win their sixth Wimbledon doubles title.

2016 Ibtihaj Muhammad is the first woman to compete in the Olympic Games wearing a hijab.

2016 Diana Taurasi wins a fourth gold medal for Team USA Basketball at the Olympic Games in Rio de Janeiro, Brazil.

2016 Simone Biles wins four gold medals at the Olympic Games in Rio de Janeiro, Brazil, making her the most decorated gymnast in history.

2019 Jill Heinerth publishes *Into the Planet: My Life as a Cave Diver*, documenting more than 7,000 diving expeditions.

2019 U.S. Women's National Team wins its fourth Women's World Cup soccer tournament, coached by Jill Ellis and captained by Megan Rapinoe, Alex Morgan, and Carli Lloyd.

Source Notes

page 5, "It's important to teach..." "WATCH: Simone Biles says she's the greatest gymnast: 'It's not out of cockiness," *USA Today*, October 14, 2019, ftw.usatoday.com/2019/10/watch-simone-biles-says-shes-the-greatest-gymnast-its-not-out-of-cockiness Accessed March 9, 2020.

page 6, "I am going to be…" Don Van Natta Jr., *Wonder Girl*. New York: Back Bay Books, 2013, p. 37.

page 8, "It would be much better…" "100 Women of the Year: 1932: Babe Didrikson," *Time*, time.com/5792780/babe-didrikson-100-women-of-the-year/ Accessed March 4, 2020.

page 8, "The Babe is here…" National Portrait Gallery, npg.si.edu/object/npg_NPG.97.211 Accessed March 6, 2020.

page 10, "Over time, I came to appreciate…" Tom Pedulla, "In Their Own Words: Julie Krone's 'Historic Ride' On Colonial Affair," Paulick Report, May 25, 2018, paulickreport.com/news/people/in-their-own-words-julie-krones-historic-ride-on-colonial-affair/Accessed March 9, 2020.

page 10, "...going from the soccer field..." Diana Taurasi, "Just a Kid from Chino,"*The Players' Tribune*, September 2, 2015, theplayerstribune.com/en-us/articles/just-a-kid-from-chino Accessed March 2, 2020.

page 11, "I am very much a daughter..." Ibid.

page 12, "It's not out of…" "WATCH: Simone Biles says ... gymnast," Accessed March 9, 2020.

page 13, "I think I'm teaching my teammates…" Alice Park, "The Olympic Gymnast Who Overcame a Drug-Addicted Mother," *Time*, June 3, 2016. time.com/collection-post/4352599/simone-biles-next-generation-leaders/

page 18, "Can you imagine…" Deborah Blagg, "Curveball: Toni Stone's Challenge to Baseball and America," Radcliffe Institute for Advanced Study, Harvard University, July 1, 2009, radcliffe.harvard.edu/news/in-news/curveball-toni-stones-challenge-baseball-and-america Accessed March 2, 2020.

page 18, "In company with…" "Indy 500 Pioneer Janet Guthrie Savors the Day She Made History," NPR, May 27, 2018, npr.org/2018/05/27/613655708/indy-500-pioneer-janet-guthrie-savors-the-day-she-made-history Accessed February 24, 2020

page 19, "Coming out of turn 4…" Speed Sport Staff, "Indy 500 Memories: Janet Guthrie," *Speed Sport*, May 24, 2016, speedsport.com/featured/indy-500-memories-janet-guthrie/ Accessed March 9, 2020.

page 20, "I know she's not out…" Adaptive Surfer Alana Nichols, "The Ocean was There When I Needed it Most," *Magic Seaweed*, December 12, 2018, magicseaweed.com/news/alana-nichols-interview-the-ocean-was-there-when-i-needed-it-most/11222/ Accessed March 8, 2020.

page 21, "I thought back to that…" 60 Minutes Sports Interview, June 28, 2016, youtube.com/watch?v=SZHBH7MYLVc Accessed March 8, 2020.

page 22, "I tell you, honey…" Elizabeth Whitley Roberson, "Under the Radar: Georgia 'Tiny' Broadwick's Parachute," *Smithsonian*, March 12, 2015, airandspace.si.edu/stories/editorial/georgia-"tiny"-broadwick's-parachute Accessed March 9, 2020.

page 28, "For me…" Matthew Stock, "The Cave Tried to Keep Us': The First-Ever Dive Inside An Iceberg," September 20, 2019, wbur.org/onlyagame/2019/09/20/jill-heinerth-cave-diving-antarctica Accessed March 9, 2020.

page 30, "They could knock me down…" Shana Renee, "Track legend Wyomia Tyus protested at the '68 Olympics and hardly anyone noticed," *ESPN Voices*, November 7, 2018, espn.com/espnw/voices/story/_/id/25211468/track-legend-wyomia-tyus-protested-68-olympics-hardly-anyone-noticed Accessed March 9, 2020.

page 33, "It was a very quiet secret…" Charlie Eccleshare, "Exclusive interview: Meet Renée Richards—sport's accidental transgender pioneer," *The Telegraph*, March 26, 2019, telegraph.co.uk/tennis/2019/03/26/meet-renee-richards-sports-accidental-transgender-pioneer/ Accessed March 9, 2020.

page 34, "My biggest achievements…" Ibid.

page 35, "Once I had my uniform…" Ibtihaj Muhammad, "Meet Ibtihaj Muhammad, First American Who'll Compete in a Hijab," (1:17) youtube.com/watch?v=ri3_hdjIX3I Acccessed February 1, 2020.

page 36, "As we marched into Rio's…" Ibtihaj Muhammad. *Proud: Living My American Dream* (Young Readers Edition). New York: Little, Brown Books for Young Readers (Kindle Edition), 2019, pp. 254–255.

p. 38, "We show up…" "Megan Rapinoe, Christen Press Speak Out After Ending US Soccer Salary Mediation," *Good Morning America*, August 15, 2019, goodmorningamerica.com/news/story/us-womens-soccer-team-ends-mediation-equal-salary-64986678 Accessed March 9, 2020.

page 39, "Eunice Kennedy Shriver: My sister Rosemary," Eunice Kennedy Shriver, Reprinted in *The Guardian*, August 12, 2009, theguardian.com/world/2009/aug/13/rosemary-kennedy-eunice-kennedy-shriver Accessed March 10, 2020.

page 39, "I would take her as a crew…" "Ibid.

page 40, "As long as you got…" Lauren A. Jones, "Women's History Month: Celebrating the NBA's First Female Referee Violet Palmer," *Los Angeles Sentinel*, March 1, 2018, lasentinel.net/womens-history-month-celebrating-nbas-first-female-referee-violet-palmer.html Accessed March 1, 2020.

page 42, "My student-athlete…" "Violet Palmer: Ball is on her court," NCAA, December 2, 2014, ncaa.org/student-athletes/former-student-athlete/violet-palmer-ball-her-court Accessed March 1, 2020.

page 42, "I was scared…" "Coordinator of Pac-12 women's basketball officiating Violet Palmer reflects on a pioneering career," YouTube, February 29, 2016, youtube.com/watch?v=E81mehZ7v1Q Accessed March 2, 2020.

page 43, I remember kicking…" Jill Ellis, "My Father's Footsteps," *The Coach's Voice*, coachesvoice.com/jill-ellis-united-states-soccer/Accessed March 9, 2020.

p. 44, "He had the ability…" Ibid.

p. 44, "Sometimes you have to cross…" "Lesley Visser's Latest 'First' Cements Her Legacy as a Trailblazer in Sports Journalism," CBS Sports, February 19, 2020, cbssports.com/general/news/lesley-vissers-latest-first-cements-her-legacy-as-a-trailblazer-in-sports-journalism/ Accessed February 29, 2020.

page 46, "Can girls do that?" Charlotte Wilder, "NFL Referee Sarah Thomas doesn't have time for your nonsense," *SBNation*, February 9, 2017, sbnation.com/2017/2/9/14510008/sarah-thomas-nfl-first-female-referee-knuck-if-buck Accessed March 9, 2020.

p. 47, "Becoming a coach…" Rebecca Stanborough, personal interview, December 12, 2019.

page 48, "A team of women…" Abby Wambach, *Wolfpack: How to Come Together, Unleash Our Power, and Change the Game*. New York: Celadon Books, 2019, p. 8.

page 50, "Fifteen to twenty minutes…" Ginny Gilder, "Our naked Ivy League protest: 'These are the bodies Yale is exploiting,'" *Salon*, April 12, 2015, salon.com/2015/04/12/our_naked_ivy_league_protest_these_are_the_bodies_yale_is_exploiting/Accessed March 10, 2020.

page 52, "Define your own course…" Mary Alice Miller, "The King, the Sailor, and the Open Sea: the Remarkable True Story of *Maiden*," *Vanity Fair*, June 17, 2019, vanityfair.com/hollywood/2019/06/maiden-documentary-tracy-edwards-sailing-interview Accessed March 1, 2020.

page 54, "I don't play…"Joseph M. Hoedel, "Teamwork—Kerri Walsh-Jennings & Misty May-Treanor," *Coaches Insider*, December 5, 2018, coachesinsider.com/volleyball/articles-volleyball/coaching-articles-volleyball/teamwork-kerri-walsh-jennings-misty-may-treanor/Accessed March 4, 2020.

page 56, "Playing Venus is like…" Serena Williams and Gayle King, "On tennis, love and motherhood," YouTube, May 22, 2017. youtube.com/watch?v=CL-SiaFuLo4 (10:30) Accessed March 5, 2020.

page 56, "In my life…" Ibid. (11:33).

Select Bibliography

Conan, Neal. "The Second Half of My Life." NPR—Interview with Renée Richards, February 8, 2007, npr.org/templates/story/story.php?storyId=7277665

Harkness, Geoff and Samira Islam. "Muslim Female Athletes and the Hijab." *Contexts*, 2011, journals.sagepub.com/doi/pdf/10.1177/1536504211427874

Heinerth, Jill. "Opinion: I am a diver who documents climate change in the Arctic. And I am running out of time." *The Los Angeles Times*, October 6, 2019, intotheplanet.com/heinerth-pens-la-times-oped-our-icy-world-is-running-out-of-time/

Hultstrand, Bonnie J. "The Growth of Collegiate Women's Sports: The 1960s." *Journal of Physical Education, Recreation & Dance* 70:4, pp. 19-23, February 25, 2013, shapeamerica.tandfonline.com/doi/citedby/10.1080/07303084.1993.10606727?scroll=top&needAccess=true#.XiTgKy2ZNN0

Miller, Mark. "Julie Krone." *Salon.com*, December 20, 2000, .salon.com/2000/12/19/krone/

Sang-Hun, Choe. "South Korea's Sea Women." *The New York Times*, March 29, 2014, nytimes.com/2014/03/30/world/asia/hardy-divers-in-korea-strait-sea-women-are-dwindling.html

Schiot, Molly. *Game Changers: The Unsung Heroines of Sports History*. New York: Simon and Schuster (Kindle Edition), 2016.

Severo, Richard. "Gertrude Ederle, the First Woman to Swim Across the English Channel, Dies at 98." *The New York Times*, December 1, 2003, .nytimes.com/2003/12/01/sports/gertrude-ederle-the-first-woman-to-swim-across-the-english-channel-dies-at-98.html

Spears, Betty. "A Perspective of the History of Women's Sport in Ancient Greece." *Journal of Sport History*, vol. 11, no. 2, 1984, pp. 32–47.

Taurasi, Diana. "Just a kid from Chino." *Players Tribune*, September 2, 2015, theplayerstribune.com/en-us/articles/just-a-kid-from-chino

Tyus, Wyomia and Elizabeth Terzakis. *Tigerbelle: The Wyomia Tyus Story*. New York: Akashic Books, 2018.

About the Author

Rebecca Stanborough is definitely not a world-class athlete, but she gets to take long walk every day because she lives, writes, and teaches in the mostly sunny state of Florida. She is the author of two other titles in the Daring Women series. obtained her BA from Agnes Scott College, a women's college in Decatur, Georgia. She also earned an MFA in Writing for Children and Adults from Minnesota's Hamline University. Rebecca is the author of four other books for young readers, and her short story "The Latter Days of Jean" appeared in the Capstone anthology Love & Profanity.

Glossary

Alpine skiing—downhill snow skiing around flagged markers

barnstorming circuit—informal baseball teams that traveled throughout the United States

discrimination—unfair treatment of a person or group, often because of race, religion, gender, sexual preference, or age

diversity—the inclusion of people of many different races, genders, classes, and religions

dojo—the facility where judo is taught

English Channel—the narrow body of water that separates England from Western Europe

Grand Slam—the four major tournaments in tennis: Wimbledon, Australian Open, French Open, and U.S. Open

hurdles—a rectangular frame runners must jump over in a race

javelin—a light spear thrown in a track-and-field sporting event

Jim Crow laws—laws that racially segregated public spaces and facilities during the early part of the 20th century in the United States

judo—the most widely practiced martial art in the world

shot put—a track-and-field event in which an athlete pushes a heavy, metal ball through the air

tournament—one or more athletic contests in which multiple athletes or teams compete for a single prize

Triple Crown—in Thoroughbred horse racing, the distinction given to a horse that wins the Kentucky Derby, Belmont Stakes, and Preakness Stakes

Critical Thinking Questions

1. Reread the sidebar on page 29 about the Korean divers called haenyeo. Find and research another unique athletic activity that is specific to a culture other than yours. Inspirations could include mountaineering, spelunking, cliff diving, wrestling, or racing. Has that activity spread to other areas of the world? Can you think of a familiar game or activity that is similar?

2. In 2018, the Girls and Sports Index Report found that girls who played sports had greater self-confidence than girls who did not. Name some reasons that might be the case. Support your answer with sources from reading or videos.

3. Several high-profile athletes have participated in political and social protests during their careers. Do you think it is a good idea for athletes to use their platforms to voice their opposition or support for political causes? Why or why not?

Further Reading

Bertovich, Yvonne. *Hidden in History: The Untold Stories of Female Athletes*. Ocala, FL: Atlantic Publishing Group, Inc., 2019.

Meadows, Michelle. *Flying High: The Story of Gymnastics Champion Simone Biles*. New York: Henry Holt and Company, 2020.

Schefff, Matt. *The World Cup: Soccer's Greatest Tournament*. Minneapolis: Lerner Publications, 2021.

Internet Sites

History of Women in the Olympic Games
https://www.olympic.org/women-in-sport/background/key-dates

Sports Illustrated Top 100 Female Athletes
https://www.topendsports.com/world/lists/greatest-all-time/women-si100.htm

World Para Athlete Organization
https://www.paralympic.org/athletics/ones-to-watch

Index